Travel Guide To Paris

Discovering the Magic of the City of Lights: A Comprehensive Travel Guide to Paris

PHILLIP S. LAMONS

This book is a work of nonfiction. All the information contained in this book is based on the author's research and personal experiences, and is presented in good faith. The author and publisher are not responsible for any errors or omissions, or for any consequences arising from the use of this information.

Table of contents

Introduction to Paris

Paris, also known as the City of Light, is one of the world's most iconic locations and an actual traveler's paradise. This beautiful town is home to some of the world's most famous landmarks, such as the Eiffel Tower, the Louvre Museum, and Notre Dame Cathedral.

Aside from its attractive architecture and wealthy history, Paris is also renowned for its world-class cuisine, high-end fashion, and vivid nightlife. Whether you are strolling alongside the

Seine River, exploring the charming neighborhoods of Montmartre or Le Marais, or admiring the city's attractive art and architecture, Paris presents an infinite array of unforgettable experiences that are sure to leave you enchanted.

If you're planning a time out to Paris, there are countless attractions and activities to pick out from. Luckily, our tour guide to Paris is right here to help you make the most of your trip. From must-see landmarks and hidden gemstones to tips on where to eat, shop, and stay, our information is your last useful resource for an unforgettable visit to the City of Light.

History

Paris is a town steeped in history, with a rich and captivating past that has formed a great deal of its present-day landscape. The earliest recognised contract in the area dates back to the third century BC, when a tribe of Gauls regarded as the Parisii established a small fishing village on the banks of the Seine River.

Over the centuries, Paris grew and evolved, becoming a middle of art, culture, and political power. In the 12th century, the city emerged as a principal middle of schooling and learning, with the founding of the University of Paris. By the 17th century, Paris had come to be the cultural capital of Europe, home to some of the world's most well-known artists, writers, and philosophers.

During the French Revolution in the late 18th century, Paris played a pivotal function in the overthrow of the monarchy and the beginning of the current French Republic. In the 19th century, the metropolis underwent a large transformation under the management of Napoleon III, with the development of grand boulevards, parks, and public squares that nonetheless outline tons of the city today.

In the 20th century, Paris noticed some of the most dramatic activities in modern-day history, such as the German occupation at some stage in World War II and the student protests of 1968. Despite these challenges, Paris emerged as a world capital of art, fashion, and culture, and remains one of the world's most beloved and iconic destinations to this day.

Culture

Paris is a city rich in culture and history. Known as the "City of Light," Paris is home to world-famous museums, art galleries, and landmarks. The Louvre Museum homes some of the most iconic works of artwork in the world, along with the Mona Lisa. The Musée d'Orsay is a must-see for those involved in Impressionist art, with works via

Monet, Van Gogh, and Renoir. Paris is additionally famous for its fashion and haute couture, with many iconic designers and fashion houses based in the city. Visitors can journey the city's lifestyle firsthand by way of exploring its many neighborhoods, each with its own special vibe and character. From the brand new Marais to the ancient Latin Quarter, there is something for everybody in the various and vibrant city of Paris.

Geography of the City of Light

Paris, also regarded as the City of Light, is positioned in the north-central place of France. The city is situated alongside the banks of the Seine River, which flows through the coronary heart of Paris and divides the town into its Left and Right Banks. The town is extraordinarily flat, with elevations ranging from 35 to 130 meters above sea level. The perfect factor in Paris is the Butte Montmartre, which presents amazing views of the metropolis from its summit. Paris is surrounded by a ring avenue known as the Périphérique, which circles the city and connects it to the rest of France. The metropolis is additionally well-connected by a network of public transportation, together with buses, metro lines, and regional trains. Paris has a mild, temperate climate, with cool winters and heat summers. The metropolis experiences moderate rainfall all through the year, with the wettest months being May and June. Paris is a beautiful and vivid city, with a rich record and tradition that attracts visitors from around the world.

Chapter 1:Planning Your Trip

First, think about the time of year you format to visit. Paris is beautiful year-round, however the climate can fluctuate greatly. Spring and fall are generally slight and pleasant, while summer can be hot and crowded, and iciness can be chilly and rainy. Keep in thought that some attractions, such as museums, may have shorter hours or be closed on sure days of the week.

Next, suppose about the place you desire to stay. Popular areas for vacationers include the Marais, Saint-Germain-des-Prés, and the Latin Quarter. Each nearby has its own unique charm and attractions, so do some research to find the one that fits your pastimes and budget. Keep in mind that lodging can be highly-priced in Paris, so book well in order to enhance the imperviousness of the fine deals.

When it comes to sightseeing, there is no shortage of things to do in Paris. The Eiffel Tower, Notre-Dame Cathedral, and the Louvre Museum are just a few of the must-see attractions. Consider buying a Paris Pass, which gives you entry to many top websites and discounts on activities and tours.

Food is a big part of Parisian culture, so be certain to indulge in some delicious French delicacies while you are there. From croissants and espresso for breakfast to steak frites and wine for dinner, there's something for everyone. Don't forget to attempt some of the local specialties, such as escargots (snails) and macarons (sweet meringue-based treats).

Finally, make time to truly wander the streets and soak up the ambiance of this beautiful city. Paris is full of charming cafes, quaint alleyways, and ancient landmarks that are fantastic discovered by using foot. And do not forget to carry an exact pair of walking shoes!

I hope this helps you diagram your day trip to Paris. Bon voyage!

Tips for choosing the best time to visit

Firstly, it's vital to reflect on the weather. Paris has a temperate climate, with moderate temperatures in the spring and fall, and hot temperatures in the summer. Winter can be chilly and rainy, however it is also much less crowded and has a sure charm. If you choose to keep away from crowds, think about journeying in the shoulder seasons of spring and fall.

Secondly, preserve the idea that some attractions, such as museums and monuments, may also have shorter hours or be closed on certain days of the week. Check the schedules earlier than you go to keep away from disappointment.

Another thing to consider is gala's and events. Paris hosts a wide variety of fairs at some point of the year, such as the Paris Jazz Festival in the summer season and the Nuit Blanche artwork festival in the fall. If you are interested in a unique competition or event, lay out your trip around it.

Price is also a consideration. Peak travel season in Paris is from June to August, and prices for flights and lodging can be greater for the duration of this time. If you are on a budget, reflect on consideration on touring in the offseason or shoulder season when expenses may additionally be lower.

Finally, suppose about your non-public preferences and interests. If you are searching for outdoor activities, spring and summer are splendid instances to visit. If you're fascinated by Christmas markets and excursion shopping, consider traveling in December. If you are a museum buff, keep in mind that many museums have free admission on the first Sunday of the month.

Overall, there is no single "best" time to visit Paris - it relies upon your non-public preferences and interests. Consider the weather, crowds, events, and prices to select the time it truly is right for you.

Getting around the city

One of the satisfactory methods to explore Paris is on foot. Many of the city's top attractions, such as the Eiffel Tower, Notre-Dame Cathedral, and the Louvre Museum, are within strolling distance of every other. Plus, walking permits you to see the city's charming neighborhoods, historic landmarks, and lovely architecture up close.

If you decide now not to walk, Paris has a tremendous public transportation system. The metro (subway) is a quick and handy way to get round the city.

There are 16 trains that cover most parts of Paris, and trains run from around 5:30 am to 1:15 am. Tickets can be bought at metro stations and permit you to transfer between trains and buses inside a sure timeframe. You can also buy a Paris Visite pass, which gives you unlimited access to the metro, buses, and trains for a set number of days.

Another option is to take the bus. Paris has a massive bus community that covers the entire city. Buses run from around 6 am to midnight, and tickets can be bought onboard or at metro stations. The advantage of taking the bus is that you can see more of the town while you travel.

Taxis and ride-sharing offerings such as Uber and Lyft are additionally accessible in Paris, however they can be more expensive than public transportation. Taxis can be hailed on the road or ordered by phone, and Uber and Lyft can be accessed via their respective mobile apps.

Finally, if you're feeling adventurous, you can rent a bike or scooter. Paris has a bike-sharing software referred to as Vélib', which allows you to hire a bike for a brief duration of time. There are also quite a few electric powered scooter-sharing services, such as Lime and Bird, that allow you to rent a scooter for a fee.

Overall, there are many approaches to get around Paris, and it is necessary to pick out the option that works excellent for you based on your budget, schedule, and preferences.

Finding the best deals on flights

Firstly, it's vital to be flexible with your journey dates. Flights to Paris can vary in price relying on the time of year and day of the week. Generally, flights for the duration of peak travel season (June to August) and major vacation trips will be extra expensive. If you're bendy with your journey dates, you can use a flight search engine like Google Flights or Skyscanner to find the cheapest options.

Another way to store cash on flights is to book in advance. Flights to Paris can be cheaper if you book various months in advance, as an alternative than ready till the closing minute. However, if you're flexible, you can also discover exceptional last-minute deals on flights to Paris.

It's also a precise thought to consider choosing airports. Paris has two essential airports, Charles de Gaulle Airport and Orly Airport, however there are also countless smaller airports in the surrounding area. If you're willing to fly into a smaller airport, you may also be capable of finding cheaper flights.

Using a tour rewards credit card can additionally help you store money on flights to Paris. Many credit cards provide rewards factors or miles that can be redeemed for flights or journey expenses. If you're a time-honored traveler, this can be an exceptional way to shop for money on flights.

Finally, signing up for electronic mail alerts from airways and tour web sites can assist you stay knowledgeable about income and promotions. Many airlines provide extraordinary offers and discounts to subscribers, so it's really worth signing up if you're planning a time out to Paris.

Overall, discovering the fantastic offers on flights to Paris requires some research and flexibility. By the usage of a mixture of these tips, you can shop cash and locate the exceptional flight options for your budget.

Accommodations

Paris has a broad range of lodging to swimsuit different budgets and preferences. Here are some picks to consider:

Hotels: Paris has a range of hotels, ranging from budget-friendly alternatives to luxury accommodations. The satisfactory areas to stay in Paris are the central neighborhoods, such as the Marais, Saint-Germain-des-Prés, and the Latin Quarter. These areas are close to many of the city's pinnacle sights and have a lively atmosphere. Some famous inn chains in Paris encompass AccorHotels, Marriott, and Hilton.

Hostels: Hostels are a great alternative for budget-conscious travelers. Paris has a range of hostels that provide shared dorms or private rooms at cheap prices. Some famous hostels in Paris include Generator Hostel, St. Christopher's Inn, and Les Piaules.

Apartments: Renting an apartment can be a right alternative if you are traveling with a crew or planning to continue to be in Paris for a prolonged length of time. There are many websites that offer momentary leases in Paris, such as

Airbnb, HomeAway, and VRBO. You can regularly locate flats that are extra low-priced than hotels, and you may have the introduced advantage of having your very own kitchen and living space.

Bed and breakfasts: Bed and breakfasts are a famous choice in Paris, especially for these searching for a more intimate and personalized experience. Many mattresses and breakfasts are placed in ancient constructions and offer a blissful atmosphere. Some

famous bed and breakfasts in Paris
consist of Le Village Hostel

Chapter 2:Top Tourist Attractions

Paris is a town with an abundance of world-famous traveler attractions. Here are some of the top points of interest to see while visiting the City of Light:

1. Eiffel Tower - No day trip to Paris would be complete without a go to the Eiffel Tower, the iconic symbol of the city. Visitors can take an elevator or climb the stairs to the pinnacle of the tower for breathtaking views of Paris.

2. Louvre Museum - One of the world's biggest and most well-known art museums, the Louvre is home to some of the most iconic works of art in history, which includes the Mona Lisa and the Venus de Milo.

3. Notre-Dame Cathedral - A masterpiece of Gothic architecture, Notre-Dame Cathedral is one of the most visited landmarks in Paris. Visitors can climb the cathedral's towers for gorgeous views of the city.

4. Champs-Élysées - Known as one of the most famous avenues in the world, the Champs-Élysées is lined with shops, cafes, and theaters, making it a famous destination for travelers and locals alike.

5. Montmartre - A bohemian nearby recognised for its artists and street performers, Montmartre is home to the famous Sacré-Cœur Basilica and affords beautiful views of Paris from its hilltop location.

6. Musée d'Orsay - Housed in a former train station, the Musée d'Orsay is home to an marvelous series of Impressionist and Post-Impressionist art, such as works by Monet, Van Gogh, and Degas.

7. Palace of Versailles - Located just in the backyard of Paris, the Palace of Versailles is a lovely example of French Baroque architecture and used to be the seat of strength for the French monarchy for centuries.

These are just a few of the many vacationer points of interest that Paris has to offer. Visitors to the City of Light will find no shortage of matters to see and do all through their stay.

Eiffel Tower to the Louvre Museum

The Eiffel Tower and the Louvre Museum are two of the most popular sights in Paris, and they're located on opposite sides of the city. Here are some choices for traveling between the two:

1. **Metro:** The Paris Metro is a convenient and less costly way to journey between the Eiffel Tower and

the Louvre Museum. You can take Line 6 from the Bir-Hakeim stop, which is placed near the Eiffel Tower, to the Palais Royal-Musée du Louvre stop, which is a quick stroll from the museum. The trip takes around 20 minutes and the value is €1.90 per ticket.

2. **Bus:** Another choice is to take the bus. The sixty nine bus is a famous route that connects the Eiffel Tower to the Louvre Museum. The trip takes around 30 minutes and the cost is also €1.90 per ticket.

3. **Taxi:** Taxis are broadly available in Paris and can be a handy option if you are traveling with bags or favor a greater blissful journey. However, they're additionally extra expensive than public transport. A taxi trip from the Eiffel Tower to the Louvre Museum can price around €15-€20, depending on traffic.

4. **Walking:** If you have the time and energy, strolling from the Eiffel Tower to the Louvre Museum can be a nice way to see the city. The walk takes

around forty five minutes and passes via some of Paris's most scenic neighborhoods, such as the Champs-Elysées and the Tuileries Garden.

Overall, there are a number of options for traveling from the Eiffel Tower to the Louvre Museum in Paris. Whether you take public transport, a taxi, or walk, you will have the possibility to see some of the city's most iconic landmarks alongside the way.

Must-see sights in Paris

Paris is domestic to some of the world's most iconic landmarks, museums, and neighborhoods. Here are some of the top must-see attractions in Paris:

1. Eiffel Tower: The Eiffel Tower is one of the most recognizable landmarks in the world, and no outing to Paris is complete without a visit. You can take the elevator to the pinnacle for gorgeous views of the city.

2. Louvre Museum: The Louvre Museum is the world's largest art museum and home to some of the most famous works of art, which includes the Mona Lisa and the Venus de Milo.

3.   Notre-Dame   Cathedral: Notre-Dame Cathedral is a masterpiece of Gothic architecture and one of the most stunning church buildings in the world. Although it suffered a devastating heart attack in 2019, it's nevertheless worth traveling for its ancient significance.

4. Montmartre: Montmartre is a bohemian neighborhood. It really is famous for its creative heritage and amazing views of the city. Don't miss the iconic Sacré-Cœur Basilica, which sits atop a hill overlooking the city.

5.   Champs-Elysées: The Champs-Elysées is one of the most famous avenues in the world and home to some of Paris's most luxurious shops, cafes, and theaters.

6. Musée d'Orsay: The Musée d'Orsay is a must-see for art lovers, providing an amazing collection of Impressionist and Post-Impressionist masterpieces.

7. Sainte-Chapelle: Sainte-Chapelle is a gorgeous Gothic chapel; it truly is well-known for its stained glass windows. It's located on the Île de la Cité, an island in the center of the Seine River.

8. Arc de Triomphe: The Arc de Triomphe is a triumphal arch that honors these who fought and died for France in the French Revolutionary and Napoleonic Wars. It's positioned at the western end of the Champs-Elysées.

Overall, Paris has so much to provide that it can be challenging to see the whole lot in one trip. However, these must-see attractions are a notable beginning point to assist you discover the beauty and records of this remarkable city.

Chapter 3:Hidden Gems

Paris is one of the most famous tourist destinations in the world, with iconic landmarks such as the Eiffel Tower, Louvre Museum and Notre-Dame Cathedral drawing hundreds of thousands of site visitors each and every year. However, there are also many hidden gem stones in the metropolis that are well worth exploring. Here are some of them:

1. Canal Saint-Martin: This picturesque waterway in northeastern Paris is a popular spot for locals to gather and relax. Take a stroll alongside the banks, experience a picnic, or even take a boat tour.

2. Musée de la Chasse et de la Nature: This small museum in the Marais district is committed to hunting and nature. It's a charming area to learn about these subjects and see some special works of art.

3. Promenade Plantée: This expanded park stretches for almost three miles above the streets of Paris. It's an awesome place to break out the hustle and bustle of the metropolis and take a leisurely walk.

4. La Pagode: This stunning cinema in the 7th arrondissement is housed in a former Buddhist temple. It monitors a mix of arthouse and mainstream films and has a lovely tea room.

5. Petite Ceinture: This deserted railway line circles the city and has been transformed into an inexperienced space. It's an awesome location to go for a stroll or bike ride and discover some hidden corners of Paris.

These are just a few of the many hidden gem stones that Paris has to offer. Exploring these lesser-known spots can supply you a complete new perspective on the metropolis and make your day trip even extra memorable.

Explore lesser-known neighborhoods

Paris is a metropolis with many frequent neighborhoods, such as the Marais, Montmartre, and Saint-Germain-des-Prés. However, there are additionally many lesser-known neighborhoods that are well worth exploring. Here are some of them:

1. Belleville: This multicultural region in northeastern Paris has a vivid arts scene, with many galleries and road artwork installations. It's also home to Parc de Belleville, which offers exceptional views of the city.

2. Butte-aux-Cailles: This small neighborhood in the 13th arrondissement has a village-like feel, with slim streets, small squares, and colorful houses. It's an amazing vicinity to wander around and discover hidden gems.

3. La Chapelle: This nearby in the 18th arrondissement is regarded for its street markets and various meals scene. It's an extremely good location to attempt some global cuisine and trip a distinct side of Paris.

4. Batignolles: This residential region in the 17th arrondissement has a relaxed, family-friendly vibe. It's home to Parc Martin Luther King, a giant green space with a lake and playgrounds.

5. Passy: This village nearby in the 16th arrondissement is frequently overlooked by tourists. It has many stunning buildings, such as the Art Nouveau-style Musée Clemenceau, and magnificent views of the Eiffel Tower.

Exploring these lesser-known neighborhoods can supply you a deeper appreciation of Paris and its many special facets. Don't be afraid to venture off the crushed direction and discover some hidden gems!

Off-the-beaten-path attractions

Paris is a city with many famous attractions, such as the Eiffel Tower, Notre-Dame Cathedral, and the Louvre Museum. However, there are additionally many off-the-beaten-path attractions that are well worth exploring. Here are some of them:

1. **The Catacombs of Paris:** This underground ossuary is home to the

remains of over six million people. It's a fascinating and truly eerie place to visit, with bones arranged in intricate patterns.

2. **Musée des Arts Forains:** This museum in the Bercy local is dedicated to fairground art and objects. It's a delightful location to explore, with antique rides, games, and attractions.

3. **Musée de la Magie:** This small museum in the Marais district is devoted to the artwork of magic. It's an exciting and interactive location to visit,

with well-known shows on the history of magic, illusions, and even a magic show.

4. **Père Lachaise Cemetery:** This well-known cemetery is the closing resting location of many famous people, consisting of Jim Morrison, Oscar Wilde, and Edith Piaf. It's a peaceable and lovely place to wander around and pay your respects.

5. **La Petite Ceinture:** This abandoned railway line circles the metropolis and has been changed into an inexperienced

space. It's a remarkable vicinity to go for a walk or bike journey and explore some hidden corners of Paris.

These off-the-beaten-path points of interest provide an exceptional point of view on Paris and its many layers of records and culture. Don't be afraid to challenge off the traveler trail and discover some hidden gems!

Local favorites

Here are some nearby favorites for your travel information to Paris:

1. Montmartre: This charming hilltop regional is regarded for its bohemian vibe, winding cobblestone streets, and gorgeous views of the city. It's a superb spot to wander and explore, with plenty of cafes, galleries, and road artists to discover.

2. Canal Saint-Martin: This picturesque waterway in the 10th arrondissement is a favorite amongst locals for its satisfied surroundings and contemporary bars and cafes. Take a stroll along the canal, revel in a picnic on its banks, or hop on a boat tour for a special point of view of the city.

3. Marché des Enfants Rouges: This historic blanketed market in the Marais is a foodie's paradise, with vendors promoting the whole thing from fresh produce and artisanal cheeses to Moroccan tagines and Japanese bento boxes. It's a super spot to seize a speedy lunch or pick out elements for a picnic.

4. Jardin des Plantes: This stunning botanical garden in the fifth arrondissement is a favorite among

Parisians for its peaceable environment and various series of vegetation and flowers. It's a magnificent spot to get away from the hustle and bustle of the city and revel in some greenery.

5.   Belleville: This multicultural neighborhood in the 20th arrondissement is recognized for its bright street art, lively markets, and diverse food scene. It's a brilliant spot to explore and discover hidden gems, from present day bars and cafes to artsy boutiques and galleries.

Chapter 4:Food and Drink

Paris is a culinary paradise, renowned for its high-quality cuisine and delectable wines. The metropolis is home to a plethora of cafes, bistros, brasseries, and restaurants, supplying an limitless array of culinary delights.

One of the must-try dishes in Paris is the French onion soup, which is a comforting and hearty soup made with caramelized onions, beef broth, and topped with a crusty bread and melted cheese. Another iconic French dish is escargots, which are snails cooked in garlic butter and served as an appetizer.

Paris also boasts an array of patisseries, where you can indulge in an assortment of pastries like croissants, macarons, and eclairs. One of the most popular patisseries in Paris is Ladurée, which is well-known for its macarons.

In addition to its food, Paris is also well-known for its wines. The city is home to some of the exceptional wine stores in the world, presenting an extensive resolution of reds, whites, and rosés from all over France. Some of the most famous wines in Paris consist of Bordeaux, Burgundy, and Champagne.

When it comes to drinks, Parisians love their coffee, and you can find a plethora of cafes serving up scrumptious espressos and cappuccinos. If you're looking for something a bit stronger, Paris is also home to some of the great cocktail bars in the world, offering innovative and innovative cocktails.

Overall, whether you're a foodie or a wine connoisseur, Paris has something to provide everyone. From its iconic dishes to its world-renowned wines, the town is a culinary destination that must not be missed.

Indulge in French cuisine

Indulging in French delicacies is an absolute ought to when touring Paris. The metropolis is regarded for its rich culinary traditions, and there are endless restaurants, bistros, and cafes where you can enjoy the exceptional French cuisine.

One of the most quintessential French dishes is the steak frites, which is a simple but delicious meal of steak and French fries. Another classic dish is coq au vin, which is a hearty stew made with chicken, crimson wine, and vegetables. And of course, no day trip to Paris would be complete besides trying the city's well-known onion soup, which is rich, savory, and oh-so-comforting.

For seafood lovers, Paris is a first-rate place to indulge in fresh oysters, which are frequently served with a glass of champagne. Another seafood dish that's famous in Paris is bouillabaisse, which is a basic fish stew that originated in the south of France.

Paris is also well-known for its pastries, and there are endless patisseries where you can indulge in an array of sweet treats. From croissants to macarons to eclairs, there is no scarcity of delicious and indulgent pastries to try.

When it comes to drinks, Paris has some of the first-rate wine in the world. From bold reds to crisp whites to sparkling champagne, there may be a wine to go well with every taste and budget. And of course, no trip to Paris would be whole barring making an attempt at the city's well-known coffee and hot chocolate, which are each prosperous and delicious.

Overall, indulging in French delicacies is a spotlight of any day out to Paris. With its prosperous culinary traditions and infinite array of scrumptious dishes, the metropolis is a meals lover's paradise that's no longer to be missed.

Croissants and macaroons to escargots and steak frites

Paris is a town that is well-known for its scrumptious food, and there are countless dishes that traffic needs to strive for throughout their stay. From sweet treats to savory classics, Paris has something to offer each palate.

Croissants and macaroons are two of the most iconic French pastries, and they can be found at bakeries and patisseries at some point of the city.

Croissants are flaky, buttery pastries that are ideal for breakfast, whilst macarons are refined and colorful cookies that come in a variety of flavors.

For those who are feeling adventurous, escargots are a traditional French dish that's well worth trying. These snails are commonly cooked in garlic butter and herbs, and they're generally served as an appetizer.

Steak frites is some other basic French dish. It truly is made with a juicy steak and an aspect of crispy French fries. This dish is simple but delicious, and it's often served in bistros and brasseries in the city.

Paris is additionally famous for its cheese, and there are limitless varieties to try. From soft and creamy brie to sharp and tangy roquefort, there's a cheese to go well with every taste.

And of course, no time out to Paris would be whole barring indulging in some wine. The city is acknowledged for its world-renowned wines, inclusive of Bordeaux, Burgundy, and

Champagne. Whether you choose red, white, or sparkling, there is a wine to suit every taste.

Overall, Paris is a food lover's paradise, with an countless array of scrumptious dishes to try. From croissants and macaroons to escargots and steak frites, the city's culinary scene is certain to satisfy even the most discerning palate.

Recommendations for the best wine bars

Paris is a town it truly is famous for its world-renowned wines, and there are infinite wine bars where you can sample some of the great vintages from throughout France and beyond. Whether you're a wine connoisseur or simply searching for a magnificent area to relax and enjoy a glass of wine, there is a wine bar in Paris that is sure to suit your taste. Here are some tips for the quality wine bars in the city:

1. La Cave des Papilles: This relaxed wine bar in the 14th arrondissement is recognised for its remarkable determination of organic and biodynamic wines. The group of workers is educated and friendly, and they're completely satisfied to make tips based on your style preferences.

2. Le Baron Rouge: This bustling wine bar in the 12th arrondissement is a favorite among locals. It's regarded for its sizable wine list, which consists of a range of inexpensive and high-end wines from throughout France. The bar additionally serves scrumptious charcuterie and cheese plates to pair with your wine.

3. Juveniles: This charming wine bar in the 1st arrondissement is a preferred among wine lovers. The bar has a cozy, rustic atmosphere, and it is regarded for its extraordinary determination of natural wines. The owners are pleasant and knowledgeable, and they're happy to make recommendations based on your taste preferences.

4. Le Verre Volé: This cutting-edge wine bar in the 10th arrondissement is regarded for its brilliant selection of herbal wines and its stylish, industrial-chic decor. The bar additionally serves scrumptious small plates and charcuterie to pair with your wine.

5. À La Ville de Rodez: This basic wine bar in the tenth arrondissement has been around since the 1930s, and it's a favorite among locals. The bar serves less costly wines from across France, and it's acknowledged for its lively atmosphere and friendly staff.

Overall, Paris is a metropolis full of outstanding wine bars, and these recommendations are simply the tip of the iceberg. Whether you're searching for a cozy, intimate surroundings or a trendy, stylish vibe, there is a wine bar in Paris that is positive to go well with your taste.

cafes

Paris is a city it is famous for its charming cafés, and there are countless locations to loosen up and revel in a cup of coffee or tea at some stage in your visit. Whether you're searching for a comfortable spot to read an ebook or a today's café to people-watch, there's a café in Paris that is certain to swim suit your taste. Here are some hints for the first-class cafés in the city:

1. **Café de Flore:** This iconic café in the Saint-Germain-des-Prés region has been around since the 1880s, and it is a favorite among locals and travelers alike. The café has a classic, Art Deco atmosphere, and it's recognised for its excellent coffee and croissants.

2. **Le Procope:** This ancient café in the 6th arrondissement has been around since 1686, and it is favored among intellectuals and artists. The café has a

cozy, standard atmosphere, and it is recognized for its wonderful coffee and pastries.

3. **Café Kitsuné:** This latest café in the Palais-Royal local is known for its stylish, minimalist decor and extremely good coffee. The café additionally serves delicious pastries and snacks, and it is a fantastic vicinity to people-watch.

4. **La Caféothèque:** This relaxed café in the Marais nearby is recognised for its top notch espresso and tea selection.

The café additionally hosts ordinary tastings and workshops, and it's an excellent vicinity to research more about coffee and tea.

5. **Café Oberkampf:** This hip café in the Oberkampf neighborhood is recognised for its super coffee and brunch menu. The café has a trendy, industrial-chic vibe, and it's a magnificent vicinity to hold out with buddies or get some work done.

Overall, Paris is a city that's full of charming cafés, and these suggestions are simply the tip of the iceberg. Whether you're searching for a classic, historical surroundings or a trendy, modern vibe, there's a café in Paris it's certain to swim suit your taste.

Brasseries

Paris is a metropolis that is famous for its brasseries, which are common French eating places that serve basic dishes like steak frites, onion soup, and escargots. These restaurants are known for their active environment and great food, and they're an outstanding area to soak up some French subculture for the duration of your visit. Here are some suggestions for the excellent brasseries in the city:

1. Bofinger: This historic brasserie in the Marais neighborhood has been around since 1864, and it is a favorite among locals and travelers alike. The brasserie has a classic, Art Nouveau atmosphere, and it is recognised for its first-rate seafood and Alsatian dishes.

2. Le Train Bleu: This grand brasserie is placed inside the Gare de Lyon teach station, and it is recognized for its ornate decor and superb food. The brasserie has a classic, Belle Epoque atmosphere, and it is a superb region to revel in a meal before catching a train.

3. Brasserie Lipp: This bustling brasserie in the Saint-Germain-des-Prés neighborhood has been around since 1880, and it's a favorite among intellectuals and artists. The brasserie has a lively, common atmosphere, and it's known for its amazing choucroute and sausages.

4. Les Deux Magots: This ancient brasserie in the Saint-Germain-des-Prés region has been around since 1885, and it's a favorite among writers and philosophers. The brasserie has a classic, Art Deco atmosphere, and it's known for its amazing espresso and croissants.

5. La Coupole: This grand brasserie in the Montparnasse local has been around since 1927, and it is a favorite amongst artists and bohemians. The brasserie has a lively, Art Deco atmosphere, and it's acknowledged for its wonderful seafood and oysters.

Overall, Paris is a city that is full of wonderful breweries, and these tips are simply the tip of the iceberg. Whether you are searching for a classic, historic ecosystem or a trendy, current vibe, there may be a brasserie in Paris it really is sure to go well with your taste.

Chapter 5:Nightlife

Paris is recognised for its bright nightlife, offering endless chances for entertainment after the sun goes down. From sublime rooftop bars to underground clubs, the town offers something for everyone.

One popular destination for tourists is the Montmartre neighborhood, known for its lively ecosystem and iconic Moulin Rouge cabaret. Visitors can revel in a show, sip cocktails, and dance the night time away in this historic district.

For a more upscale experience, the Champs-Élysées boasts a range of ultra-modern bars and clubs. From special nightclubs to elegant rooftop lounges, this vicinity presents a style of Parisian glamor.

For a greater relaxed evening, the Marais local is a tremendous option. This bohemian district is home to a range of bars and restaurants, from comfy wine bars to active beer gardens.

Overall, Paris's nightlife scene is diverse and exciting, with alternatives for each style and budget. Visitors are positive to discover some thing to go well with their fashion and make unforgettable recollections in the City of Lights.

Cabarets to jazz clubs

Paris has lengthy and storied records when it comes to nightlife entertainment, which include cabarets and jazz clubs. Here are some of the top options for traffic looking to journey the city's shiny nightlife scene:

Cabarets:

- Moulin Rouge: One of the most iconic cabarets in the world, the Moulin Rouge in Montmartre gives a staggering spectacle of music, dance, and acrobatics.

- Lido de Paris: Another legendary cabaret, the Lido de Paris dazzles audiences with its glamorous revues and problematic stage shows.

- Crazy Horse: Known for its sensual and avant-garde performances, the Crazy Horse cabaret is a must-see for those searching for a special and unforgettable experience.

Jazz Clubs:

- **Duc des Lombards:** Located in the coronary heart of the city, this jazz membership hosts top musicians from around the world in an intimate and blissful atmosphere.

- **Sunset/Sunside:** This famous jazz club in the ancient Marais district presents live music each and every night, ranging from normal to experimental jazz.

- **Caveau de la Huchette:** This ancient jazz membership in the Latin Quarter has been a fixture of the Parisian jazz scene since the 1940s, and nevertheless draws crowds with its lively song and dance floor.

Whether you are looking for a night of glitz and glamor or a more laid-back night time of live music, Paris has no scarcity of selections when it comes to cabarets and jazz clubs.

Explore the vibrant nightlife scene in Paris

Paris is acknowledged for its shiny nightlife, and the metropolis affords a vast vary of alternatives for site visitors searching to explore its after-dark scene.

Here are some recommendations for experiencing the nice of Paris's nightlife:

- **Start with aperitifs:** In Paris, the hours between work and dinner are acknowledged as l'heure de l'apéro, a time for socializing over drinks and small bites. Join the locals in a present day bar or satisfied wine cave for a pre-dinner drink and some people-watching.

- **Head to a cabaret:** Paris is well-known for its cabarets, which offer a special blend of music, dance, and theater. From the iconic Moulin Rouge to the avant-garde Crazy Horse, there may be a cabaret to suit every taste.

- **Check out the jazz clubs:** Paris has a wealthy jazz history, and the city is home to a number of legendary clubs. Catch a live performance at one of the intimate venues in the Marais or Saint-Germain-des-Prés neighborhoods.

- **Get your dance on:** For those searching to hit the dance floor, Paris has no scarcity of nightclubs and discos.

From the chic rooftop bars of the Champs-Élysées to the underground golf equipment of the Bastille, there is a birthday party scene for each and every taste.

- **Take a midnight stroll:** One of the great ways to ride the magic of Paris at night time is to take a leisurely stroll through the city's illuminated streets. The Eiffel Tower, Notre-Dame, and the Seine river are particularly lovely when lit up after dark.

Overall, Paris's nightlife scene is various and exciting, with something for absolutely everyone to enjoy. Whether you're looking to catch a show, dance the night time away, or absolutely soak up the city's lively atmosphere, Paris has lots to offer after the sun goes down.

Chapter 6:Shopping

Paris is a shopper's paradise, with an extensive range of preferences for each and every finances and style. Here are some of the pinnacle shopping destinations in the city:

- **Champs-Élysées:** This iconic avenue is home to some of the world's most well-known luxury brands, such as Louis Vuitton, Chanel, and Dior. Even if you're not in the market for high-end fashion, it's really worth a stroll down the boulevard to take in the sights.

- Le Marais: This ancient district is known for its modern-day boutiques and old shops. From dressmaker clothing to one-of-a-kind accessories, there may be something for everybody in Le Marais.

- Rue Saint-Honoré: Another high-end shopping destination, Rue Saint-Honoré is domestic to flagship stores for manufacturers such as Hermès, Yves Saint-Laurent, and Cartier. Even if you are now not planning to buy, it is well worth a go to admire the window displays.

- Galeries Lafayette: This massive branch store is a must-visit for any client in Paris. With over 70,000 rectangular meters of retail houses and a huge range of brands and products, it's handy to spend hours shopping the aisles.

- Flea markets: Paris has a number of lively flea markets, where you can discover the whole thing from antique apparel to vintage furniture. The Marché aux Puces de St-Ouen is one of the largest and most popular, with over

2,500 vendors spread out over 7 hectares.

Whether you're searching for luxurious fashion, unique finds, or old treasures, Paris has no shortage of buying options. Just be positive to convey cozy footwear and plenty of euros!

Best boutiques

Paris is known as the trend capital of the world, and for exact reason. The metropolis is home to some of the most iconic fashion houses and boutiques in the world. For these searching to keep at some of the great boutiques in Paris, here are a few recommendations:

1. **Colette:** This is a must-visit boutique for everyone fascinated in fashion. Colette is known for its special collection of apparel, accessories, and splendor products from some of the world's most sought-after designers.

2. **Merci:** One of the most popular boutiques in Paris, Merci elements an eclectic collection of clothing, furniture, and accessories. They additionally have

an in-house café, making it the best spot for a buying break.

3. **The Broken Arm:** This boutique presents a cautiously curated determination of clothing and accessories from both hooked up and rising designers. The Broken Arm additionally has a café on-site, serving up scrumptious coffee and pastries.

4. **L'Eclaireur:** With numerous places all through Paris, L'Eclaireur is a boutique that is now not to be missed. They offer a diverse variety of clothing,

accessories, and home goods, all with a special and modern aesthetic.

5. **Isabel Marant:** Known for her cool style, Isabel Marant has a number of boutiques at some stage in Paris. Her collections function a combination of bohemian and urban styles, with a focus on terrific fabric and interest in detail.

Markets

Paris is a town famous for its markets, presenting site visitors a risk to keep for a huge variety of products, from fresh produce to old clothing. Here are some of the nice markets for buying in Paris:

1. Marché aux Puces de Saint-Ouen: This is one of the largest and most famous flea markets in the world, providing over 2,000 companies promoting the entirety from antiques to old clothing. It's a notable vicinity to find special and one-of-a-kind items.

2. Marché d'Aligre: This bustling market in the twelfth arrondissement is recognized for its clean produce, however it also presents a variety of other products, including cheese, meat, and flowers. There are additionally numerous cafes and restaurants nearby where you can grab a chunk to eat.

3. Marché des Enfants Rouges: This is the oldest included market in Paris, a relationship dating back to the seventeenth century. Today, it's a famous spot for foodies, with providers promoting the whole thing from Moroccan tagines to Japanese sushi.

4. Marché Bastille: Located in the 11th arrondissement, this market is open twice a week and has over 100 providers selling clean produce, seafood, cheese, and more. There are additionally quite a few garb and accessory stalls, making it a super spot for a day of shopping.

5. Marché Saint-Germain: This market in the 6th arrondissement has a greater upscale feel, with carriers selling connoisseur cheeses, wines, and pastries. There are additionally a number of restaurants and cafes close by where you can enjoy a leisurely meal.

Department stores for fashion

Paris is renowned for its luxury department stores, which are a must-visit for fashion lovers. Here are some of the satisfactory department stores for trend buying in Paris:

1. **Galeries Lafayette:** This iconic branch shop is located on Boulevard Haussmann and is a Parisian institution. The store facets a wide variety of clothier clothing and accessories, inclusive of luxury brands like Chanel,

Dior, and Hermès. There's additionally a gourmand food corridor and a rooftop terrace with wonderful views of the city.

2. **Le Bon Marché:** This upscale branch save in the 7th arrondissement is known for its elegant and sophisticated vibe. The store elements a mix of high-end and contemporary fashion, as well as beauty products, domestic goods, and gourmet food. There's additionally an in-house bookstore, artwork gallery, and restaurant.

3. **Printemps:** Another famous branch store on Boulevard Haussmann, Printemps presents a broad range of dressmaker fashion and accessories, as well as beauty merchandise and home goods. The preserve is known for its attractive Art Nouveau architecture, which was recently restored to its unique glory.

4. **BHV Marais:** This department shop in today's Marais region affords a mix of fashion, homeware, and splendor products. The safe has an extra laid-back vibe than some of the

different branch shops in Paris, with a center of attention on cutting-edge and informal fashion.

5. **La Samaritaine:** After years of renovation, this iconic branch save on the banks of the Seine River has recently reopened. The store elements a combination of luxury and current fashion, as nicely as beauty products, domestic goods, and a rooftop terrace with attractive views of the city.

Antiques

Paris is a haven for antique lovers, with several markets, fairs, and shops offering an extensive array of antique and vintage items. Here are some of the high-quality locations for antique buying in Paris:

1. Marché aux Puces de Saint-Ouen: This big flea market on the outskirts of Paris is domestic to over 2,000 providers selling the entirety from old clothing to antique furniture. The market is divided into quite a few sections, each with its personal specialty, making it effortless to locate precisely what you are searching for.

2. Village Saint-Paul: This charming neighborhood in the Marais is home to countless antique shops and galleries, promoting the entirety from old earrings to antique furniture. It's a notable area to browse and discover special finds.

3. Marché aux Timbres et Monnaies: This market specializes in stamps and coins, but additionally gives a range of other vintage and antique items, which includes postcards, books, and memorabilia. It's positioned in the coronary heart of Paris, close to the Notre Dame cathedral.

4. Passage Verdeau: This blanketed passage in the 9th arrondissement is home to various antique dealers and bookshops, selling the whole lot from old posters to antique furniture. It's a hidden gem in the heart of Paris, with a blissful and intimate atmosphere.

5. L'Isle-sur-la-Sorgue: While now not technically in Paris, this small town in the south of France is acknowledged for its antiques markets, which draw site visitors from all over the world. The markets are held several times a 12 months and function over 300 companies selling everything from antique furniture to old clothing. It's worth the outing for vintage lovers.

Souvenirs

Paris is a city that is rich in tradition and history, and there are limitless souvenir selections for those searching to take a piece of Paris home with them. Here are some of the satisfactory souvenirs to store for in Paris:

1. **Eiffel Tower replicas:** The iconic Eiffel Tower is one of the most popular souvenirs in Paris. You can find miniature replicas in various sizes and materials, from keychains to problematic metal sculptures.

2. **Macarons:** These refined French pastries are a must-try for the duration of a visit to Paris, and they also make terrific souvenirs. You can take home boxes of macarons from well-known patisseries like Ladurée and Pierre Hermé.

3. **Perfume:** Paris is recognised for its perfumes, and there are various retail outlets and manufacturers to pick out from, along with Guerlain and Diptyque. You can choose from a range of scents and bottle sizes to find the ideal souvenir.

4. **Art prints:** Paris is home to some of the world's most famous art museums, and you can locate prints of well-known works of art, like the Mona Lisa and Starry Night, in souvenir stores throughout the city.

5. **Books:** Paris is a literary city, and there are a number of bookshops that offer a variety of books in French and English. You can discover traditional French literature, as nicely as books about Paris and its history.

6. **Fashion accessories:** Paris is acknowledged for its fashion, and you can locate a range of accessories like scarves, hats, and gloves in memento stores at some point of the city. You can also save for fashion designer fashion in

branch shops like Galeries Lafayette and Le Bon Marché.

7. **Postcards and magnets:** These classic souvenirs are a gorgeous way to take into account your day out to Paris. You can discover postcards and magnets featuring famous landmarks like the Eiffel Tower and Notre Dame Cathedral.

Chapter 7:Day Trips

Paris is no longer only a lovely city, but it is also surrounded by charming towns and countryside areas that are perfect for day trips. Here are some of the great day journeys to take from Paris:

1. Versailles: Located simply 30 minutes outside of Paris by means of train, Versailles is famous for its lovely palace and gardens. Visitors can tour the palace, stroll through the gardens, and even watch the well-known fountain show.

2. Giverny: This small village, located about an hour's backyard of Paris, was once home to the famous impressionist painter Claude Monet. Visitors can tour Monet's house and gardens, which inspired many of his paintings.

3. Champagne region: The Champagne region is positioned about two hours backyard of Paris and is home to some of the world's most well-known champagne houses, including Moët

Palace of Versailles or the Champagne region

The Palace of Versailles and the Champagne vicinity are two of the most popular day trips from Paris, each supplying a unique experience for visitors.

Palace of Versailles:

Located simply 30 minutes in the backyard of Paris with the aid of trains, the Palace of Versailles is an attractive example of French Baroque structure and is one of the most well-known palaces in the world. The palace was once at first constructed as a looking hotel for Louis XIII however used to be extended and renovated over the years by means of Louis XIV and his successors. Today, visitors can tour the palace and its opulent rooms, which include the famous Hall of Mirrors, and stroll through the amazing gardens, which are adorned with fountains, sculptures, and manicured lawns. The palace also hosts a range of occasions during the year, together with musical performances and fireworks displays.

Champagne region:

Located about two hours outside of Paris, the Champagne vicinity is home to some of the world's most famous champagne houses, which include Moët.

Chapter 8:Practical Information

Here are some realistic data for the journey guide to Paris:

1. Language: The legitimate language of Paris is French, however many human beings speak English as well.

2. Currency: The currency used in Paris is the Euro (€). You can change your forex at banks or trade offices.

3. Weather: Paris has a temperate climate with mild winters and moderate summers. The satisfactory time to go is at some stage in spring (April-June) or fall (September-November) when the climate is pleasant.

4. Transportation: Paris has a great public transportation system, which includes buses, metro, and trains. You can buy a Paris Visite omit that approves limitless tours on public transport for a set period.

5. Food: Paris is well-known for its scrumptious cuisine, including croissants, baguettes, and cheese. You can locate many cafes and eating places around the metropolis serving French cuisine.

6. Accommodation: Paris has a huge range of accommodation options, consisting of hotels, hostels, and apartments. It is endorsed to strengthen throughout the peak season.

7. Safety: Paris is usually a secure city, however it is constantly important to be conscious of your surroundings and take precautions to avoid pickpocketing and other crimes.

8. Tourist attractions: Paris is home to many famous traveler attractions, along with the Eiffel Tower, the Louvre Museum, and Notre-Dame Cathedral. It is advocated to purchase tickets in advance to avoid lengthy queues.

Tips for staying safe

Here are some sensible tips for staying safe in Paris:

1. **Be aware of your surroundings:** Stay alert and conscious of your surroundings at all times, specifically in crowded areas or vacationer hotspots. Keep an eye on your belongings and be cautious of pickpockets.

2. **Stick to well-lit areas:** Stick to well-lit areas and keep away from taking walks on my own in dimly lit or secluded areas, mainly at night.

3. **Use legit taxis or ride-sharing services:** If you want to use a taxi or ride-sharing service, make certain to use

a reputable one. Avoid unmarked taxis and always confirm the driver's identification and car small print before getting in.

4. **Keep your valuables safe:** Keep your valuables such as passport, cash, and deposit playing cards in a tightly closed place such as a hotel safe. Avoid carrying large amounts of cash with you.

5. **Beware of scams:** Be aware of frequent scams such as human beings presenting to assist you with your

baggage or asking for directions. Always be cautious and preserve your wits about you.

6. **Stay up to date on contemporary events:** Keep yourself updated on any contemporary occasions or security warnings in the area via checking nearby news sources or government tour advisories.

By following these tips, you can help make sure a secure and fun day out in Paris.

Getting around

1. Use public transportation: Paris has an extremely good public transportation system, inclusive of the metro, buses, and trains. It's low priced and efficient, and you can purchase tickets at stations or through cell apps.

2. Consider a hop-on-hop-off bus tour: If you're a tourist, a hop-on-hop-off bus tour can be a magnificent way to see the city's essential attractions. These excursions typically encompass audio commentary and enable you to get on and off at a range of stops.

3. Walk or bike: Paris is a very walkable city, and taking walks is a superb way to discover the unique neighborhoods and get some exercise. You can also rent bikes from a number of bike-sharing services for the duration of the city.

4. Taxis and ride-sharing services: Taxis and ride-sharing services are readily available in Paris, and can be a proper alternative for getting around if you are brief on time or touring with luggage.

5. Rent a car: If you plan on traveling outside of the city or exploring rural areas, you may additionally choose to think about renting a car. However, keep in mind that riding in Paris can be challenging, with heavy visitors and slim streets.

By thinking about these distinct options, you can pick out the excellent way to get around Paris primarily based on your desires and preferences.

Navigating cultural differences

When traveling Paris, it is vital to be aware of cultural variations in order to have an effective and fun experience. Here are some sensible tips:

1. **Greetings:** In Paris, it is familiar to greet people with a handshake or a kiss on each cheek, even if you've simply met. This is a sign of appreciation and friendliness.

2. **Dress code:** Parisians have a tendency to dress extra formally than in different parts of the world. Avoid wearing shorts, flip flops or revealing apparel when journeying museums, churches or restaurants.

3. **Language:** While many Parisians communicate English, it is always polite to research some basic French phrases. Try to make an effort to communicate the language, even if it is just a few words.

4. **Dining:** When dining in Paris, it is necessary to consider that foods are generally longer and extra leisurely than in other components of the world. Waiters will now not rush you to finish your meal, so take your time and experience the experience.

5. **Tipping:** Tipping is not as common in Paris as it is in the United States. However, it's nonetheless accepted to depart a small tip of 5-10% for magnificent service.

By being respectful of cultural differences, you'll be capable of fully recognizing all that Paris has to offer.

Conclusion

In conclusion, Paris is a town that surely lives up to its reputation as the City of Lights and one of the most romantic and beautiful cities in the world. From the amazing structure and art to the delicious delicacies and charming neighborhoods, Paris has something to provide for everyone. Whether you are a first-time traveler or a pro traveler, there is usually something new to find out in this bright city. So don't hesitate to e book your trip to Paris and trip all that this magical city has to offer!

Final thoughts on visiting Paris

In conclusion, traveling Paris is really a once-in-a-lifetime journey that will leave you with unforgettable memories. From the iconic Eiffel Tower to the charming cafes and boutiques, Paris is a town that has captured the hearts of people from all over the world. While it can be overwhelming to navigate the town at first, taking the time to explore its more than a few neighborhoods and points of interest is well really worth the effort. Whether you are interested in art, history, or certainly relaxing and playing the Parisian lifestyle, there is something for each person in this beautiful city. So go ahead and format your day trip to Paris - you might not be disappointed!